MONSTER
Dump Trucks

by Nick Gordon

BELLWETHER MEDIA • MINNEAPOLIS, MN

Note to Librarians, Teachers, and Parents:

Blastoff! Readers are carefully developed by literacy experts and combine standards-based content with developmentally appropriate text.

Level 1 provides the most support through repetition of high-frequency words, light text, predictable sentence patterns, and strong visual support.

Level 2 offers early readers a bit more challenge through varied simple sentences, increased text load, and less repetition of high-frequency words.

Level 3 advances early-fluent readers toward fluency through increased text and concept load, less reliance on visuals, longer sentences, and more literary language.

Level 4 builds reading stamina by providing more text per page, increased use of punctuation, greater variation in sentence patterns, and increasingly challenging vocabulary.

Level 5 encourages children to move from "learning to read" to "reading to learn" by providing even more text, varied writing styles, and less familiar topics.

Whichever book is right for your reader, Blastoff! Readers are the perfect books to build confidence and encourage a love of reading that will last a lifetime!

This edition first published in 2014 by Bellwether Media, Inc.

No part of this publication may be reproduced in whole or in part without written permission of the publisher. For information regarding permission, write to Bellwether Media, Inc., Attention: Permissions Department, 5357 Penn Avenue South, Minneapolis, MN 55419.

Library of Congress Cataloging-in-Publication Data

Gordon, Nick.
  Monster dump trucks / by Nick Gordon.
    pages cm. – (Blastoff! readers: Monster machines)
  Summary: "Developed by literacy experts for students in kindergarten through grade three, this book introduces big dump trucks to young readers through leveled text and related photos"–Provided by publisher.
  Audience: K-3
  Includes bibliographical references and index.
  ISBN 978-1-60014-938-2 (hardcover : alkaline paper)
  1. Dump trucks–Juvenile literature. I. Title.
  TL230.15.G6735 2014
  629.224–dc23
                                                                    2013006838

Printed in the United States of America, North Mankato, MN.

Table of
Contents

Monster Dump Trucks!

Giant dump trucks help builders and **miners** move heavy loads.

Every dump truck has a **cab**. This is where the driver sits.

cab

The **bed** is
the large box
behind the cab.
It holds sand,
dirt, and more.

bed

Off-Road Dumpers

The largest dump trucks do not travel on roads. They are too big.

Some dump
trucks are taller
than houses.

The tires can
be taller than
a person!

People use
ladders to
climb into these
dump trucks.

Biggest Dump Trucks

The biggest
dump trucks have
king-size beds.

They carry up to 400 **tons**. That is the weight of 200 cars!

Glossary

bed—the part of a dump truck that carries loads

cab—the part of a dump truck where the driver sits to operate the machine

miners—workers who collect resources from the ground

tons—units of weight; one ton equals 2,000 pounds (900 kilograms); the average car weighs about 2 tons.

To Learn More

AT THE LIBRARY

Gilbert, Sara. *Dump Trucks*. Mankato, Minn.: Creative Education, 2009.

Glaser, Rebecca Stromstad. *Dump Trucks*. Minneapolis, Minn.: Jump!, 2013.

McClellan, Ray. *Dump Trucks*. Minneapolis, Minn.: Bellwether Media, 2007.

ON THE WEB

Learning more about dump trucks is as easy as 1, 2, 3.

1. Go to www.factsurfer.com.

2. Enter "dump trucks" into the search box.

3. Click the "Surf" button and you will see a list of related Web sites.

With factsurfer.com, finding more information is just a click away.

Index